I0159604

THE JESUITS

BY

Rev. JOSEPH RICKABY, S.J.

JESUIT SAINTS
SS. IGNATIUS, FRANCIS XAVIER, FRANCIS BORGIA,
ANDREW BOBOLA, ALOYSIUS, STANISLAUS

REVISED EDITION

Thirty-Fourth Thousand

CATHOLIC TRUTH SOCIETY

38/40 ECCLESTON SQUARE, LONDON, S.W.1 & 28A ASHLEY PLACE

Branches at Liverpool, Manchester, Birmingham, Cardiff, Brighton,
Newcastle, and Derby

Price Twopence

Front cover of the Catholic Truth Society edition of 1931

THE JESUITS

Rev. Joseph Rickaby, S.J.

BooksUlster

The text of this book has been taken from *The Jesuits* by Joseph Rickaby, published by The Catholic Truth Society, London, 1931.

This edition published by Books Ulster in 2016.

Typographical arrangement © Books Ulster.

ISBN: 978-1-910375-42-6 (Paperback)

The cover background illustration is *Carte geographique de la Nouvelle France* (Map of New France) by Samuel de Champlain, 1612. The Jesuits established a number of missions there in the early 17th Century.

I. Life in the Society of Jesus

Whoever enters the Society of Jesus, or any other Religious Order, does so of his own free will. There is no conscription, we are all volunteers. The intending novice of the Society is examined by four priests appointed for the purpose. They report separately to the Provincial, whose approval is necessary for his admission. The usual age of admission is from about eighteen to twenty-five. Some are admitted as laybrothers. They are put through no course of studies, and are for the most part employed in domestic duties. But they are not servants; they are religious equally with the rest, and wear the religious habit. The proportion of laybrothers to other members of the Society in 1911 was about 25 per cent.; in England and Scotland it is somewhat less. The laybrothers, notwithstanding their name, do not wander about in lay society, but live in the religious house with the rest of their brethren—they are only called "laybrothers" because they will never be priests. In the Society of Jesus their official name is Temporal Coadjutors. A person admitted to the Society to study for the priesthood is called a Scholastic Novice. The noviceship lasts two years. When the two years are over, he becomes a Scholastic, and is known as such up to the date of his ordination to the priesthood. Thus, in a large house of the Society there are priests (or Fathers), scholastics, and laybrothers. It is a mistake to call all who are not priests "novices." The novices are not scattered through the various houses, but are all kept together in one house, under a superior called the Master of Novices. The house is called the Novitiate. The Novitiate for England and Scotland is Manresa House, Roehampton, S.W. Little or no study is done in the Novitiate. The rules of the Society are explained to the novices; their obedience and humility are tested by the performance of menial offices in the house and manual labour in the garden. They are encouraged to put every confidence

St. Ignatius of Loyola, painted by Peter Paul Rubens, circa 1620

in their Master, to tell him of their difficulties and dislikes.

He studies them individually, and advises them to leave or continue in the Society. But they are free to leave at any time, even against his advice; as the Society also is free to dismiss them, even against their will. Every care is taken not to admit to their vows either the unfit or the unwilling, nor is there any attempt to put old heads on young shoulders. The novices are allowed reasonable recreation and exercise, and are well fed. They are made to perform the Spiritual Exercises of St. Ignatius in full. This is called the Long Retreat, and lasts a month. When the two years are elapsed, the novice who is satisfied with the Society, and with whom the Society is satisfied, is admitted to his simple vows of poverty, chastity, and obedience. The first vow binds him to have nothing of his own, and only to use things with the explicit or tacit permission of his Superior. Thus one who has taken the vow of poverty can have neither money, food, nor clothes, except what his Superior allows him. At the same time his Superior is bound in justice to supply him with all bodily necessaries and decencies according to his state, and would speedily be removed from office if he failed in this duty. The practical effect of the vow of poverty is that the religious has not money about him to spend as he pleases.

In taking the vow of chastity, the novice engages not to marry, and to observe in all things what Catholics call the sixth and Protestants the seventh commandment. The vow of obedience binds one to do what the Superior commands according to the rule and custom of the Society, yet so that nothing ever be commanded that is sinful, contrary to the law of God or the just law of the State. Thus no vow of obedience can ever bind anyone to steal a sixpence, to tell even a small lie, to plot against the Civil Government, or to smuggle contraband goods, such as spirits and tobacco, into the country without paying duty. If a Government were absolutely to forbid the importation of breviaries and crucifixes, or the landing of missionaries, a religious might be commanded to contravene that prohibition, for the law would not be just—the Church would consider it beyond the competence of the civil legislator. Happily, such laws are not now made in England, but they were made 250 years ago, and then Jesuits broke them with a good conscience.

By these simple vows the Scholastic is tied to the Society, so that he cannot now go away without a dispensation. The power of dispensation, or even of dismissal, rests with the chief Superior of the Society, called the General. A Scholastic is not dismissed except for gross misconduct, or faults of character such as to disqualify him for the Society. If he and his Superiors otherwise think that he is not in the right place, a dispensation from his vows is granted. Illness does not involve dismissal, unless the invalid himself wishes it. Practically, a Scholastic is never retained against his own fixed will.

After the vows, the noviceship being now ended, the Scholastic goes through two years' study of literature and elementary mathematics; or else, if possible, the Society affords him the benefit of some University training. The Society has a liking for Universities. Its first ten members were Masters of Arts in the University of Paris. In England the Society held by the London University for many years; it now sends some of its best students to Oxford. After literary studies come three years of philosophy, diversified by mathematics and physical science. The house of philosophy and theology in England is Heythrop College, Chipping Norton, Oxon. When they leave their philosophy, they are sent to teach boys at some of the schools or "colleges" of the Society. There are nine such schools in England and Scotland: they are Stonyhurst, near Blackburn; Mount St. Mary's, near Chesterfield; Beaumont, near Windsor—these three are boarding schools: also the following day schools:—St. Francis Xavier's, Liverpool; Wimbledon College, Wimbledon; St. Ignatius', Stamford Hill, North London; St. Aloysius', Garnethill, Glasgow; the Catholic College, Preston;

the Catholic College, Leeds. A Scholastic who does well as a teacher will be kept at the work for several years. Then he goes to begin his course of four years' theology.

At the end of the third year he is ordained, and at the end of each year of philosophy and theology, an oral examination is held of half an hour or an hour, and finally of two hours. These examinations are of increasing difficulty. Failure in any of them involves some sort of abridgement of the course of studies, as also inability to hold the offices of Provincial or General.

When the studies are at length over, the young priest is sent to what is called the "tertianship," namely, to spend a third year in the exercises in which he was engaged as a novice. This is intended to counteract any loss of religious spirit which he may have contracted in the ardour of study. When that is over, he makes what is known as his "Last Vows," or "Solemn Vows of Profession." These vows are in matter the same as before—poverty, chastity, and obedience, along with a fourth vow to go anywhere at the Pope's bidding, even though His Holiness does not provide travelling expenses. These vows are called "solemn" because they are less easily dispensed from than "simple vows." A "Professed Father" cannot be dismissed from the Society except for the gravest cause, and by authority of the Holy See. Those who have taken their Last Vows are employed either on home missions (in which case their work is not unlike that of the secular clergy in England and Scotland), or on foreign missions, or in teaching in the Society's schools, or in government. The cardinal point in this final phase of life is that the subject may be sent to live in any house of the Society within the "Province" at the discretion of the "Provincial." Higher Superiors excepted, a Jesuit has no fixity of tenure.

It may as well be remarked here that there are no "crypto-Jesuits," no "Jesuits in plain clothes," nor "Jesuits in disguise." A Jesuit house is known all over the town, and Jesuits all live in their own houses, unless the Government shuts up the house and disperses the inmates. A Jesuit never goes in disguise, except in countries where he is threatened with the gallows or imprisonment, if recognized; in that case he is fain to imitate the persecuted Saints of old, of whom St. Paul says "They walked about in sheepskins" (*Heb.* xi. 37). Out of doors a Jesuit priest or scholastic in this country is dressed like a secular priest; a laybrother in the same way but without the Roman collar. Indoors the priests and scholastics wear a gown with wings; the laybrothers, a similar gown without wings. There are no female Jesuits anywhere. There is no affiliation to the Society except in this sense, that sometimes a person is given a special participation in the prayers of the Society without being a member or living in its houses, or being subject to its control. Every Jesuit is of course a Catholic. All authority within the Society is derived from the Pope. A Pope approved the Society in 1540: a Pope suppressed it in 1773: another Pope restored it in 1814. Secular priests and Jesuits say Mass at the same altar, and preach the same faith.

II. Government of the Society

The supreme authority in the Society of Jesus is the General Congregation; that alone can make laws. There are, however, fundamental points which the Congregation cannot alter, but only the Pope. The General Congregation does not sit permanently. It meets for the election of the General, and may meet at certain other times, as presently to be explained. In practice, the Society is not ruled by Congregations nor Committees, but by individuals. The supreme individual ruler is the General, who is elected for life, and resides ordinarily in Rome. The present General is the Very Rev. Vladimir Ledóchowski, a Pole, elected in 1915. Resident with the General is a Council of Assistants, also elected by the General Congregation. They are his advisers, but not his colleagues; the General governs by his own sole authority. He appoints the Superiors of Provinces and of Colleges, and is in regular correspondence with them. All extraordinary issues are decided by him. He is bound, however, to rule according to the Constitutions of St. Ignatius Loyola, Founder of the Society, the decrees of General Congregations, and the traditions of the Society. Next to the General in authority are the Provincials, one in each Province, appointed by the General, but not for life, and removable at his pleasure. The usual tenure of a Provincial's office is from three to eight years.

The Society at present consists of forty Provinces and Vice-Provinces, six in Italy, six in Germany, four in France, nine in Spain and Spanish-speaking countries, five in English-speaking countries with Belgium, six in America, and four in Slavonia. The grand total of Jesuits as reported up to first of January, 1930, is 21,678, The returns of the English Province of the same date show a total of 837—the population of a large village, men of all ages from eighteen to eighty. To the ordinary Jesuit the Provincial is much the most important of Superiors. The General he never sees, and rarely hears of; but with the Provincial he has an interview every year, at the annual visitation, and for all important and unusual affairs has recourse to him. It is also by the Provincial that he is moved from place to place in the Province, and has his office assigned. Each Province is divided into "Colleges." There are fifteen Colleges in the English Province, each College a place of education, with a group of parochial residents attached. Each College is normally presided over by a Rector, who holds his appointment from the General for periods of from three to nine years. The Rector's second in command, appointed by the Provincial, is called the Minister. As the General has his Assistants, so every Provincial and every Rector has his Consultors, who aid him with their advice, which he takes or not as he sees fit. Unlike the older Religious Orders, the Society of Jesus has no chapter meetings, and does not sing the Divine Office in choir. Nor has it any statutory corporal austerities, such as fasting and abstinence, beyond what is enjoined by the Church on all the faithful.

Every three years there meets what is called the "Provincial Congregation." This consists of the Provincial, the Rectors, and the senior Professed Fathers of the Province, up to the number of forty in all. This Congregation has no legislative authority, but elects one Proctor, whom it sends to Rome with any petitions which it may wish to present to the General; likewise it passes a vote whether it wishes the General Congregation to be convened or not. If the majority of the Proctors wishes it, the General is obliged to convene the General Congregation. That body consists of the Provincial and two deputies of each Province, the deputies being elected in a Provincial Congregation in which fifty Fathers sit. When assembled, the General Congregation is supreme, even to the deposing of the General, as was nearly done to Father-General Thyrsus Gonsalez some two hundred years ago. That, however, is an extreme and unlikely proceeding. Usually,

Portrait of Thyrsus González (1624-1705)

the General Congregation meets only when the General is dead, its meeting being then a necessity for the election of his successor.

Financially, the Society may be described as built in watertight compartments. Each house is a financial unit, and one house is not responsible for the debts of another; nor is it usual to transfer a member from one Province to another. To nearly every Province is attached some foreign mission. Thus to England are attached missions in South Africa and the West Indies.

The important thing in government is not the paper theory but the traditional working. The following remarks appeared in *The Month* in 1898, and apply particularly to the government of the Society of Jesus: "What saves individual liberty in a Religious Order, and keeps the members of the body supple and elastic in their work, is not so much the machinery of the constitution as the spirit in which the constitution works. The Heads of the Order have ample powers of command, but are very slow to draw upon them. They hardly ever put out all their authority. They tread softly, handle gently, and are loth to proceed *pro imperio*. Rules are not applied without the unction of charity and what theologians call ἐπιείκεια (epieikeia) or regard for circumstances. Superiors and their elder subjects have grown up together from early youth, and know one another's ways better often than brothers of the same family. They have common interests, common ideals, and are on the easiest of speaking terms. No government is at once so gentle and so firm, so considerate towards the individual, and at the same time so attentive to the general good, as the government of a healthy Religious Body."

III. Idea of the Society

"Jesuit," like "Christian," was originally a nickname (*Acts* xi. 26: I *Pet.* iv. 16). The Church has adopted the name "Christian" and received it as an official designation. Not so the name "Jesuit." It may be used without offence, and is used by members of the Society speaking of themselves, but in all official documents the only name for the Body is *Societas Jesu;* and the individuals are *socii* (thus S.J. is *socius Jesu,* "companion of Jesus"): or if the document is the Society's own, they are called *Nostri* ("Ours"). The expression "The Order of Jesus" betrays one who is a stranger to the Society; Jesuits do not speak of the "Order," but of the "Society." In France, Spain, and Italy, they call it the "Company," the name being taken in a military sense, and so St. Ignatius understood it. This leads us to the "Spiritual Exercises" of St. Ignatius.

These embody the fundamental idea upon which the Society of Jesus was originally founded and is still based. No one knows the inner mind of the Society of Jesus who is a stranger to the Spiritual Exercises; they are a continuous course of meditations, lasting properly for thirty days, but usually shortened to eight. They are divided into four "weeks." In the first "week" the great truths of the end of man, sin, hell, death, and judgement are considered. The remaining three "weeks" answer to the triple division of the mysteries of the Rosary, Joyful, Sorrowful, and Glorious. The core of the Exercises is in the second "week"—notably in two famous meditations, one on the Kingdom of Christ, the other on the Two Standards of Christ and Lucifer. The upshot of these meditations is that the "exercitant" is led, not necessarily to join the Society, nor any Religious Order, nor to become a priest, but anyhow to resolve on a chivalrous following of Christ, to advance His kingdom, "not of this world" (*St. John* xviii. 36) with "arms of warfare not fleshly" (2 *Cor.* x. 5: *Eph.* vi. 11-17), and to turn those arms in the first place against himself, to the overthrow of self-love, self-will, and self-interest, so far as worldly comforts and worldly reputation are concerned. It is possible to serve a great cause in such a way as to make the cause, at least at times, secondary to one's own gain, and one's own fame, and one's own advancement and position. Many men have served their country in this spirit, and so have sometimes injured her; and St. Paul complains of men who "seek their own, not the things of Jesus Christ" (*Phil.* ii. 21). The Society, founded on the Spiritual Exercises, endeavours to serve Christ in quite another spirit, a spirit of detachment and disinterestedness: hence the accusation of her enemies, that the Society crushes the individual. It is not for one moment pretended that every deliberate choice of every Jesuit is guided by the principles of the Spiritual Exercises; but every member of the Society owns to those principles, and more or less makes them the rule of his life. No Jesuit has notably swerved from them and prospered in his vocation. To the carrying out of those principles is to be attributed all the spiritual success which the Society has achieved; nay, under the blessing of God, whatever temporal success may have been vouchsafed to it.

Every member of the Society of Jesus is bound by obedience under mortal sin to take no active part in secular politics. It is undeniable that in the sixteenth and seventeenth centuries some Jesuits were greatly involved in political designs, in the interests of religion, as they conceived it. These efforts gave great dissatisfaction to other members of the Society, and on the whole were not crowned with success: hence the stringent prohibition, which has been mentioned, was issued. It is still binding, and at the present day is well observed. When a General Election comes off in this country, no one thinks of inquiring on which side the influence of the Jesuits is thrown. Neither Liberal nor Conservative leaders, nor any of their numerous agents, ever apply to the Society for its support. They recognise that the Society of Jesus is a cypher in politics throughout His Majesty's dominions. A Jesuit will often have his political sympathies, derived not from the Society but from his parentage; but when Jesuit is conversing with Jesuit, politics are hardly ever mentioned, except for amusement. Mercutio's "A plague o' both your houses" is a usual Jesuit sentiment towards the Montagues and Capulets of the political arena. The "political priest," whatever his merits, is not a Father of the Society of Jesus.

The following "Sum and Scope of our Constitutions" is printed in the Rule of the Society; it is an ideal—like other ideals, but imperfectly realised, still, recognised and reverted to: "Men crucified to the world, and to whom the world itself is crucified, such does the plan of our life require us to be: new men, I say, who have stripped themselves of their own sentiments to put on Christ; dead to themselves, to live to justice: who, as St. Paul says, in labours, in watching, in fasting, in knowledge, in long-suffering, in sweetness, in the Holy Ghost, in charity unfeigned, in the word of truth, show themselves the ministers of God, and by the arms of justice on the right hand and on the left, through glory and ignominy, through evil fame and good fame, through prosperity and adversity, hasten by forced marches to their heavenly country themselves, and urge others thither by every means and effort in their power."

IV. Unpopularity of the Society

In speaking of the odium that has gathered round the name "Jesuit," it must be borne in mind that the Society always has had many kind friends and warm admirers. We must not treat of "the winter of our discontent" as though there were no "glorious summer" to set it off. It is impossible to set down any one circumstance as though that were the whole cause or the chief cause of the unpopularity of the Society. Nor is it possible to enumerate all the circumstances which together make up the cause, nor to appreciate the relative weight assignable to one circumstance or another as elements in this causation. Sufficient to say that some of the concurrent circumstances seem to be the following.

(*a*) The Society was founded in the sixteenth century, an age of religious animosities. From the martyrdom of Edmund Campion to Oates's plot— that is, for a century—the Jesuit traversed England and Scotland in fear of his life. He acted the "artful dodger": poor man, what else could he do? The evil name has clung to him; and the cloud, under which he was born, has never dispersed. (*b*) Englishmen are intensely disliked in many quarters of the world; they flatter themselves that this dislike is the penalty of their commercial success. There may be some analogous reason operative in the dislike for Jesuits. (*c*) It would be hard to maintain that nothing has ever been done by Jesuits, reasonably to breed dislike. In a Society that is now more than three centuries old, and once numbered 22,000 members, no wonder if argus-eyed searchers of records find some over-clannishness, some forgetfulness of the proper subordination of the Society to the common good of the Church, some bitter resentment of wrong, some unhappy excess of timidity; for they who fear too often come themselves to be feared and suspected. The fifth petition of the Lord's Prayer is for the use of all individuals and all corporate bodies of Christians, even the Society of Jesus. (*d*) There is a tradition that the Founder of the Society prayed that it might never be without persecution. St. Ignatius thought that the close following of Christ, and the active maintenance of His cause in the world, necessarily entailed persecution. He was moved by texts like the following:—"Ye shall be hated of all men for my name's sake. But when they persecute you in this city, flee ye into another. The disciple is not above his master, nor the servant above his lord. If they have called the master of the house Beelzebub, how much more them of his household" (*St. Matt.* x. 22-25). "Blessed are ye, when men shall hate you, and banish you, and reproach you, and cast out your name as evil, for the Son of Man's sake" (*St. Luke* vi. 22). "If the world hate you, know ye that it hated me before you. If you had been of the world, the world would love its own: but because you are not of the world, but I have chosen you out of the world, therefore the world hateth you. If they have persecuted me, they will persecute you also: if they have kept my word, they will even keep yours" (*St. John* xv. 18-20). "And all who wish to live godly in Christ Jesus, shall suffer persecution" (2 *Tim.* iii. 12).

V. Doctrine of the Society

"And not as we are spoken ill of, and as some say that we teach, let us do evil that good may come of it: whose condemnation is just" (*Romans* iii. 8).[1]

I will briefly consider the allegation that the Society of Jesus teaches the maxim that the end justifies the means, or that we may do evil that good may come of it, St. Paul notwithstanding. The maxim is nothing short of heresy, being in manifest contradiction with Holy Scripture. The allegation then amounts to this, that in the Catholic Church a large religious body, absolutely subject to the Holy See, has been teaching for centuries and still teaches a gross heresy. The allegation is an insult, not merely to the Society of Jesus but to the Holy See and to the whole Catholic Church.

A foreigner gets hold of some maxim of English law. He puts his own construction upon it. He will consult no living English lawyers. He is heedless of their reclamations and repudiations. The law absolutely must be and shall be according to the foreign ruling of it; and having ruled the point in his own peremptory, unauthorized way, this foreigner rounds upon the English bench and bar, and cries fie upon them for their wicked pronouncement. This is Cardinal Newman's parable of the Russian lecturing on the axiom of the British constitution that the King can do no wrong. Similar is the treatment of the maxim that "to whom the end is

---

[1] The article on Jesuits in the *Encyclopaedia Britannica* has been re-written and much improved, but it is still inaccurate on the variety of Jesuit vows. The grade of Spiritual Coadjutor is final, not intermediate to that of Professed Father, any more than the B.Sc. at Oxford is intermediate to the M.A. The matter is stated correctly in *Chambers's Encyclopaedia*, ed. 1895. See *Does the End Justify the Means?* by the Rev. J. Gerard, S.J. C.T.S. 2d.

lawful, to him the means are lawful," at the hands of persons of the Protestant Alliance type. The maxim is not a very common one in the Jesuit schools, not very common and not very wise, being open to misconstruction; and when it is brought out, it is immediately guarded by distinctions manifold to prevent abuse. Really it is a very harmless maxim, when explained as we are careful to explain it. It means that there is always (at least in the abstract) a right way of doing a right thing: when the thing is right, you may take the right, proper, and pertinent way of doing it, if that way is open to you. Thus, if it is right to eat beef, it is right to kill oxen and cook them; if it is right to swim, it is right to go into the water with due observance of decency; if it is right to hang a murderer, it is right to bring him to trial in a competent court; if it is right to have children, it is right to beget them in lawful wedlock; if it is right to shoot an enemy in war, it is right to manufacture gunpowder and exercise oneself at the rifle butts. This is the way that Jesuits and all reasonable men understand the maxim.

In every Catholic treatise on morals, Jesuit or otherwise, there is laid down at starting a certain *thesis,* founded upon St. Thomas Aquinas (*Summa Theologica,* i.-ii., qq. 18, 19, 20). The *thesis* is this: "The morality of a human act is determined by its object, its end, and its circumstances." As soon as the beginner has mastered this *thesis,*—and the *thesis* is fundamental in our system—he has mastered the truth which the *thesis* explicitly contains, that the end does not justify the means. There are two books extensively used in English-speaking Jesuit schools at this date, both by the same Jesuit author. The one is entitled *Aquinas Ethicus,* being, so far as it goes, a translation of St. Thomas Aquinas; the other is the volume on *Moral Philosophy* in the series of *English Manuals of Catholic Philosophy* (Longmans). In the Index to *Aquinas Ethicus* (vol. ii. p. 449) I find: "End does not justify the means." Following up the reference, I find these statements, translated from St. Thomas,

DVO COPIOSISSIMI
INDICES
Diu multumque hactenus ab omnibus desiderati

SVMMÆ THEOLOGICÆ
DIVI THOMAE AQVINATIS.

NVNC DENVO CORRECTIORES,
ac maxima diligentia in singulis suis partibus locupletati dantur,
ut pagina versa demonstrat.

IN QVORVM CALCE COLLOCATVS
est Catalogus authorum & librorum omnium, quos
D. THOMAS per totum opus citat.

VENETIIS, MD XCVI.

Apud Iuntas.

Title page to 1596 edition of 'Summa Theologica'

and evidently accepted by the translator (vol. i., pp. 75, 76)—

> We must further observe that, for a thing to be evil, one single defect suffices; but for a thing to be absolutely good, one single good point suffices not, but there is required an entirety of goodness. If therefore the will be good both in point of having a proper object and of having a proper end in view, the interior act is consequently good. But for the exterior act to be good, the goodness of will, which comes of the intention of the end, does not suffice. If the will be evil either from the intention of the end or from the act willed, the exterior act is consequently evil. A good will, as signified by a good tree, must be taken as having goodness at once from the act willed and from the end intended. Not only does a man sin by the will when he wills an evil end, but also when he wills an evil act.

Let us hear the translator speaking in his own person. At p. 31 of his *Moral Philosophy,* he lays down the *thesis* above mentioned, which he puts in this form: *"The morality of any given action is determined by three elements, the end in view, the means taken, and the circumstances that accompany the taking of the said means."* At p. 32 he explains what is said of the means taken:—

> If morality were determined by the end in view, and by that alone, the doctrine would hold that the end justifies the means. That doctrine is false, because the moral character of a human act depends on the thing willed, or object of volition, according as it is or is not a fit object. Now the object of volition is not only the end in view, but likewise the means chosen. Besides the end, the means are likewise willed. Indeed, the means are willed more immediately even than the end, as they have to be taken first.

He adds some further explanation on pp. 47, 48:

> Thus an end entirely just, holy, and pure, purifies and sancti-
> fies the means, not formally, by investing with a character of
> justice means in themselves unjust, for that is impossible—
> the leopard cannot change his spots,—but by way of elimi-
> nation, removing unjust means as ineligible to any purpose,
> and leaving me only those means to choose from which are
> in themselves just. With means in themselves indifferent,
> the cause is otherwise. A holy and pious end does formally
> sanctify those means, while a wicked end vitiates them. I beg
> the reader to observe what sort of means are here in ques-
> tion. There is no question of means in themselves or in their
> circumstances unjust, as theft, lying, murder, but of such
> indifferent things as reading, painting, singing, travelling.
> Whoever travels to commit sin at the end of his journey,
> his very travelling, so far as it is referred to that end, is part
> of his sin: it is a wicked journey that he takes. And he who
> travels to worship at some shrine or place of pilgrimage, in-
> cludes his journey in his devotion: the end in view there
> sanctifies means in themselves indifferent.

Finally, at pp. 207, 208, the author attempts a sort of mathemat-
ical demonstration, of which I give only the conclusion:

> When the distance, difference, or distinction between the
> evil circumstance and the means comes down to nothing at
> all, and the evil thing actually is the very means taken, then
> an infinite urgency of end in view would be requisite to the
> using of that means: in other words, no end possible to man
> can justify an evil means.

There is a Greek drama in which the hero complains: "My crimes
are the things done to me rather than the things I have done."

May not the Society of Jesus use this quotation in reference to this matter of the end justifying the means? No calumny seems to be too monstrous, no call on credulity too vast, no thrice-convicted error too impudent in re-asserting itself, provided these wicked means serve the pious end of putting down Jesuits and Jesuitry.

A scarcely less obnoxious name than Jesuitry is Casuistry. Jesuits hold no monopoly of casuistry. Every priest who hears confessions must be a casuist: nay, in a certain sense, every lawyer is a casuist. Casuistry is the study of cases of law. The lawyer studies the law of the State: the confessor studies all law, divine and human, in so far as it is binding upon consciences. Not that he expects to forecast every case that may arise; for cases are inexhaustible. He must have knowledge of law, principles, common sense, and experience; all these are exercised in the study of cases of conscience. When a new case arises, the confessor meets it, arguing from like to like—from cases something like it to this particular case now before him, which he has not met with before—ever keeping a hold upon principles and common sense.

Men do not commonly consult their lawyer to find out a heroic and generous line of conduct, but a line which will be safe, within the letter and practice of the law. This the lawyer has studied, and this he points out. No man blames him for that. A confessor has many grades of penitents. Some are full of ardour and generosity: these he trains in the path of self-sacrifice, to do far more than they are bound to do, to wait on God's will of good pleasure, rather than on His will of absolute command. Other penitents he gets, who will barely consent with much pressing and urging to do as much as they are bound to do under grave and serious obligation—obligation which cannot be neglected without mortal sin. It is the confessor's duty to be able to lay down accurately the lines of such obligation. Upon these he takes his stand, and says to this man of little good will: "This I must absolutely require; short of this I must refuse you absolution, and forbid you to approach Holy Communion; this is the extreme boundary line, which you cannot transgress without becoming an enemy of God, or within which you must re-enter to be restored to the friendship of God." To be able to draw that boundary line is part of the art of casuistry. When a casuist says "This is barely permissible," he does not invite you to it; when he writes "This is the least you can do," he does not advise you to do no more.

Moreover, books of casuistry are like books of medicine. They are not meant for the reading of the general public. Malicious persons may cull extracts from them, and publish them, and do harm thereby: but that harm is chargeable, not on the professional man, be he medical man or priest, but on that malicious circulator of what is not written for the many. Dirt has been defined as "matter out of place." What is not dirt in the pages of a pathological or casuistic treatise, because there it is in its right place, becomes dirt in these prurient and malicious reprints, unfit matter for the untrained mind.

VI. General History of the Society of Jesus

The Society was founded in the University of Paris in the year 1534, and was approved by Paul III in a Bull dated 1540. The ten first Fathers, all Masters of Arts in that University, were St. Ignatius Loyola, Founder and first General, St. Francis Xavier, the celebrated missionary, Blessed Peter Favre, James Lainez, the second General, Alphonsus Salmeron, Simon Rodriguez, Nicholas Bodadilla, Claude Le Jay, John Codure, Paschase Brouet—the last three were Frenchmen, the others Spaniards, with the exception of Favre, a Savoyard. The first intention was to live in the Holy Land. A war with the Turks having made this impossible, they turned their eyes to the organization of the Society as it still exists, according to the written Constitutions of the Founder. The Bull *Regimini* of Paul III in 1540 gave the Society existence as a Religious Order. St. Ignatius died in 1556. By that time the members of the Society were numerous in Italy, where it continued to flourish, almost without a check, till the suppression. In Spain the Society found a powerful support in Francis Borgia, third Duke of Gandia, a member of the family to which Popes Calixtus III and Alexander VI belonged. He joined the Society himself, became its third General, and was afterwards canonized. The Jesuit Schools of Theology in Spain attained to celebrity, producing men of the stamp of Suarez, Vasquez, and Molina, who are still recognized theological authorities. In Portugal the Society found a protector in King John III. The College of Coimbra made a great name for itself. The works of the Coimbricenses, commentators on Aristotle, make part of the vast literature that has gathered round the name of that philosopher. The Society flourished most in Italy, Spain and Portugal, Belgium, and Southern Germany.

The College at Louvain was ennobled by the name and teaching of the theologian Leonard Lessius. St. Peter Canisius was the first Provincial of Germany, appointed by St. Ignatius. It may be doubted whether the Society has rendered any better and more lasting service to the Church than the preservation of the Faith in Central and Southern Germany. In France, down to the present day, the Society has had a chequered career. At its first entrance into that country it was vehemently opposed by the very institution which had given it birth, the University of Paris. The University regarded it as an educational rival; the Parliament of Paris also was its implacable enemy. It was also an objection that so many of its members were Spaniards. But it found favour with the first three Bourbon Kings, Henry IV, Louis XIII, and Louis XIV. Its bitterest enemies were the Jansenists, a sect who started in France a heresy not unlike Calvinism, condemned by Clement XI and other Popes. The struggle of Jansenist and Jesuit went on for a century and a half. Both combatants perished in the crisis that culminated in the first French Revolution. In the hearing of confessions and the assigning of penances the Jansenists were exceedingly severe, and reproached the Jesuits with laxity in those matters. From that contention emanated the Provincial Letters of Pascal,[1] a sword of keen satire and misrepresentation, under the keen edge of which the Society still bleeds.

Away from the acrimony of theological controversy, the Society found a happy field of labour in the foreign missions, principally in India, Japan, China, Canada, and Paraguay. Francis Xavier, the chief companion of St. Ignatius, laboured ten years in India and Japan with results hard to parallel in the annals of missionary enterprise. In Southern India in the century following, Robert de Nobile lived the hard life of the Brahmins, to gain

---

[1] See *Pascal's "Provincial Letters"* by Hilaire Belloc. C.T.S. 2d.

French tapestry depicting Jesuit astronomers with Chinese scholars

souls for Christ. Rudolph Aquaviva (brother of Claude Aquaviva, fifth and most celebrated of the successors of St. Ignatius in the Generalship of the Society) lived for years at the court of the

19th Century painting of Jesuit martyrs in Paraguay—Saints Juan del Castillo, Roque González and Alfonso Rodríguez

Great Mogul, and was subsequently martyred. The first quarter of the seventeenth century witnessed in Japan the opening of one of the most systematic and cruel persecutions which the Church has ever endured. The persecution burst with exceptional fury upon the Society of Jesus in that country, and there were many martyrs. In Canada, many French Jesuits were martyred with horrible torments by the Iroquois and other wild tribes of Indians.

Nor was persecution wanting in China. There however at one time the Society met with a singular measure of success, imperial favour, honour, and distinction. Fathers Ricci (died in 1610), Schall, and Verbiest, by their astronomical lore delighted the Emperor, and lived with the honours of mandarins. The last years of the Society's work in China, previous to the suppression, were clouded with an unhappy dispute among the Catholic missionaries about what were known as the Chinese Rites. It was thought that the Jesuits had been too complacent in allowing the Chinese to pay honour to their departed ancestors, even, it was said, beyond the verge of idolatry.

The most wonderful of all Jesuit missions was that of Paraguay in South America. The lives of the Europeans out there were so scandalous, that, to save the natives from corruption, as also from being reduced to slavery, the Jesuits obtained leave from the Crown of Spain to have the missions of Paraguay (a land where there is much water and no gold) given over to their sole charge, European traders being excluded. The natives were gathered into what were called Reductions. The Bishop and the Royal Inspectors retained the right of inspecting the Reductions. In every Reduction there lived two Jesuits. Each Reduction was self-supporting and autonomous. This system worked until, in the eighteenth century, Paraguay was ceded by Spain to Portugal. The Society was thereupon suppressed, and since that date neither Christianity nor civilization among the natives of Paraguay has been what it was in the days of the Jesuits.

17th Century portrait of Father Henry Garnet

In the British Isles, until the nineteenth century, the Society had no large houses of its own, and no settled footing in the country. Its members wandered as persecuted missionaries, in danger of their lives: or, later, lived quietly as chaplains to Catholic county families. The only gleam of sunshine in their fortunes was for a few months under James II. The first two Jesuit missionaries, Blessed Edmund Campion, the Martyr, and Robert Parsons, landed in England in 1580. Campion was hanged, drawn, and quartered at Tyburn, December 1, 1581; Parsons escaped to the Continent. The Venerable Henry Garnet was put to death in 1606, on a false charge of being accessory to the Powder Plot. Five or six Jesuits were executed under Charles II for that tale of imposture and credulity, Oates's Plot. No Jesuits have been put to death in this country since. In Ireland, Salmeron, one of the first ten Fathers, went as Papal envoy. The wanderings and persecutions of the Irish Jesuits have been similar to those of their English brethren. As was to have been expected, Jesuits found no mercy from Cromwell.

Fathers Hay, Creighton, and other Jesuits went as secret envoys to the Court of Mary Stuart, in the days when Mary in Scotland was the one hope of Catholicism. It does not appear that they effected much: certainly they harmed none; some of their reports remain, and are valuable historic evidence. The cruel martyrdom of the Blessed John Ogilvie, S.J., in the reign of James I, for no other cause than that of the Catholic Faith, is one of the glories of the Scottish Church.

The Society of Jesus was suppressed by Pope Clement XIV in the Brief *Dominus ac Redemptor,* July 21, 1773. It had already been expelled from Portugal in 1759, from France in 1764, from Spain and Naples in 1767. Previously to these calamities the Society had numbered 22,589 members, residing in 24 professed houses, 669 colleges, 176 seminaries, 61 novitiates, 335 missionary residences in Catholic countries, and 275 missionary stations in infidel countries or in the Protestant States of Europe. A "professed house," it

Portrait of Pope Clement XIV

may be remarked, is a house where professed Fathers live and no scholastics. It is founded on a basis of severe poverty, and depends for its whole support on alms. At the present day the Society finds it impossible to maintain more than one "professed house".

The Brief *Dominus ac Redemptor* was, as the Society might have said in Shakespeare's words to the Pope who issued it, "A heavy sentence, my most sovereign liege, and all unlooked for from your highness' mouth." It reduced the Society and its works for the time being to dust. It contains a long enumeration of complaints that had at various times and places been made against the Society of Jesus. At the same time, a careful reader will observe that the Brief rehearses these complaints historically, as complaints that in point of fact have been made; and by no means so clearly pronounces, if indeed it pronounces at all, that these complaints, all or most of them, were justified in fact. The Brief has nothing whatever to do with doctrine: it is a disciplinary and administrative measure: Papal Infallibility does not enter into it. All that a Catholic, reading the Brief needed to believe was that the Society was truly and canonically suppressed in all countries where the Brief was promulgated. It was never promulgated in Russia, whither the Jesuits flocked under the protection of Catherine II. Pius VII formally recognized the existence of the Society in Russia in 1801; in Sicily in 1804; and finally by the Bull *Solicitudo omnium ecclesiarum,* August 7, 1814, he restored the Society of Jesus throughout the world; that day is regarded as the birthday of the "New" Society, as September 27th—the date of the Bull *Regimini*—is of the "Old." "Old" and "New" together make one Society of Jesus.

The halo of romance has not surrounded the brow of the "New" Society. Its members have been and are for the most part either quiet scholars keeping school, or authors writing books that are not generally read, or missionaries doing the uneventful work of a Catholic priest on the mission, whether at home or abroad. Martyrdom has not been plentiful, as of old in the days of Elizabeth and James, and Iroquois Indians, and infuriated bonzes and Brahmins. In the Paris Commune, and in the Chinese mas-

1845 engraving of Jesuits being expelled from St. Petersburg in Russia

sacres, some Jesuits lost their lives. There has not been room for a theologian of the celebrity of Suarez and Molina, mankind having gone in quest of other lore. Still, the New Society has produced theologians of mark in Rome, as Perrone, Franzelin, Mazzella. Paraguay Reductions are of the number of modern impossibilities, but something of the Reduction system may some day be found practicable where Jesuits are at work on the banks of the Zambesi. Christian and Catholic Majesties have become a rare species, and I do not know that any of those who survive has a Jesuit confessor. Pères Lachaise and Le Tellier are no more at the ear of kings. No General of the Society in the nineteenth century has attained the European reputation of Claude Aquaviva. There are no Jansenists, happily, left to wrangle with, except in Holland, some few, quiet and obscure. There is no Elizabeth for any modern Robert Parsons, on religious grounds, to seek to dethrone. English, Scotch, and Irish Jesuits no longer live in hiding-holes, or say Mass with closed doors and sentinels posted at early hours in the morning. The Jesuit of the twentieth century is, I hope, not a vulgar, but certainly a prosaic and matter-of-fact sort of person. His politics are of the commonplace order, and little enough of that: he touches no secret springs of information; he tells you that he has not read even the whole of last week's *Tablet*. Plain, prosy natures of this sort are the despair of the historian. With a world clamouring for history—yes, veracious modern history of the doings of the Jesuit,— whither shall the conscientious chronicler betake himself? There is legend enough to be sure, thrice confuted legend (neither legend nor confutation to be entered here), but even that legend touches chiefly the Old Society, and finds less matter of invention in the New.

There remains a history of petty persecutions of the Society in various European countries during the nineteenth century—persecutions painful and vexatious, but not exalted into the regions of the visibly heroic by the rope and knife of Tyburn, the dungeons of His Majesty's Tower, or the watering-can sprinkling the live Jesuit's bare skin with the sulphureous burning waters of Japanese Ungen. From Spain, then, the Jesuits were expelled for five years, 1820-1825; for nine more, 1835-1844; again, 1854-1858; again in 1868; and after all came back.

The vicissitudes of the Society in nineteenth-century France are too numerous to record: who to-day takes interest in the doings of the Government of Louis-Philippe? There was an expulsion in 1880, inconvenient enough, yet somewhat of the nature of a farce. The invasion of Garibaldi in 1860 drove the Society from Naples and Sicily: then followed the proceedings of the Italian Government in the years succeeding the capture of Rome in 1870,—spoliation and expulsion, though not so complete as in France.

Directed by Prince Bismarck, the Government of the German Emperor took alarm at the definition of Papal Infallibility by the Vatican Council. Considering the Jesuits to have been main advisers of that measure, Bismarck by law in 1873 broke up all their houses in the territory of the Empire, and forbade their corporate existence, and indeed their doing any work as Jesuits there at all. Since then, Jesuits have done better in Germany. They have a large school at Feldkirch, in what was Austrian territory, which draws many German boys, and another school in Holland. They keep houses of study for the scholastics of the Society on Dutch territory, close to the German frontier. For many years the German Fathers at Ditton Hall were widely known in the North of England, and welcomed for the aid they were ever ready to render to the secular clergy; they have since removed to Holland. There are also Provinces of Austria, of Hungary, of Czechoslovakia, Jugoslavia, and Poland.

Further to enter into the fortunes of the Society in the twentieth century belongs not to history but to prophecy. An idea is entertained in some quarters that the Society of Jesus is an old-

Painting, circa 1925, of Jesuit martyrs in Canada in 1649

world institution, a machine that has served its time but is now antiquated, incapable of adaptation to modern requirements— something therefore that ought to be broken up, as impeding the progress of the Church and the world. The Society is the servant of the Holy See; and to the Holy See finally it belongs to decide whether the Society of Jesus shall be maintained in place or discharged. "To its own master it standeth or falleth," and, continuing the Apostle's words, its children will say in hope, "it shall stand, for God is able to make it stand" (*Rom.* xiv. 4). Like other large bodies, the Society may be expected to contain timid and over-cautious men, also impetuous and rash men, besides some men of discretion. Like other large bodies, it is also slow to move and averse to change. The division into Provinces, however, enables changes to be made according to local needs. In England and America, and no doubt elsewhere too, the Society shows by its deeds no slight readiness to keep up with the times. An educational body must ride with the time; for a contemplative Order there is no time; it rests with gaze fixed upon the eternity of God.

Ever and anon the word "suppression" is borne on whispering winds to the Jesuit's ear. But he does not fear it; only the Pope can canonically suppress him. As a bone once broken and set again is said to grow stronger, so the Society is in some measure more secure for having been once suppressed. The years in which the Society lay in abeyance were not happy years for the Church. The corrupt monarchies, mainly instrumental in that suppression, have perished or have changed. The Society has no quarrel with the advancing force of democracy. Nowhere does it flourish better than under the free institutions of Great Britain and America. While the breath of true liberty inspires the French Republic, it will flourish there also. The individual Jesuit—at least the English-speaking variety of the species—is cheery and confident of the future. The mutter of the storm occasionally reaches his ear: but things are very different in England and Scotland under Victoria and Edward and George from what they were under Elizabeth and James; and those old times can scarcely be brought back by any recrudescence of bigotry. Besides supernatural considerations of the Divine protection, which never failed his ancestors, though it spared them not the conflict, the Jesuit has, from an earthly stand-point, some of the proverbial vivacity of the cat with nine lives.

O passi graviora, dabit Deus his quoque finem.

(Harder has been the past,
So present grief shall end.)

www.ingramcontent.com/pod-product-compliance
Lightning Source LLC
Chambersburg PA
CBHW060636030426
42337CB00018B/3384